Gluten-Free

DESSERTS

3

What is Gluten?

Gluten is a protein that is found in wheat, rye, and barley. There are many reasons people avoid gluten. Some people are allergic to wheat itself while others may have a sensitivity to gluten and just feel better when they avoid it. The most serious is Celiac Disease, in which the body produces an autoimmune response after eating gluten. The only way to manage this condition is to follow a strict gluten-free diet.

No More Bread? No Pasta?

At first, going gluten-free may appear to be rather limiting. Fortunately, there are many more delicious foods on the gluten-free list than on the forbidden list. There are also more and more products, from cereals to baking mixes to pastas, which are now being formulated in gluten-free versions. These days you'll find them not just in health food stores and online, but also on the shelves of most major supermarkets.

Some Good News

Spotting hidden gluten in processed foods is a lot easier now thanks to the FDA's Food Allergy Labeling Law that went into effect in 2004. Since wheat is a common allergen, any product that contains wheat or is derived from it must say so on the label. That means formerly questionable ingredients, such as modified food starch or maltodextrin, must now show wheat as part of their name if they were made from it (for example, "wheat maltodextrin"). Be aware that this ONLY applies to foods produced in the US and Canada. Imports are a different matter.

More Good News

Look at your dietary restrictions as an opportunity to try new foods. Add quinoa and chickpea flour to your cupboard. Use corn tortillas to make sandwiches or lasagna. You'll find easy recipes in this book that are so delicious you'll forget that they're gluten-free. Healthy eating may actually be easier without gluten, too. Adding more fresh produce to your meals, eating less processed food and avoiding refined flour are all steps to a better diet for anyone.

Gluten-Free Flour Blends

While there are many products that are now readily available in the supermarkets, they can be rather expensive. We have provided a basic flour blend that can be prepared in bulk and kept on hand for use at any time. Please refer to this when preparing many of the recipes in this book.

Gluten-Free All-Purpose Flour Blend

- **1 cup white rice flour**
- **1 cup sorghum flour**
- **1 cup tapioca flour**
- **1 cup cornstarch**
- **1 cup almond flour or coconut flour**

Combine all ingredients in large bowl. Whisk to make sure flours are evenly distributed. The recipe can be doubled or tripled. Store in airtight container in the refrigerator.

Makes about 5 cups

Classic Brownies

$1/4$ **cup soy flour**

$1/4$ **cup cornstarch**

$1/2$ **teaspoon baking soda**

$1/4$ **teaspoon salt**

$1/2$ **cup (1 stick) butter**

1 **cup packed brown sugar**

$1/2$ **cup unsweetened cocoa powder**

$1/2$ **cup semisweet chocolate chips**

1 **teaspoon vanilla**

2 **eggs**

1. Preheat oven to 350°F. Spray 8-inch square baking pan with nonstick cooking spray.

2. Combine soy flour, cornstarch, baking soda and salt in small bowl; mix well. Set aside.

3. Melt butter in large saucepan over low heat. Add brown sugar; cook and stir until sugar is dissolved. Remove from heat; sift in cocoa and stir until combined. Stir in flour mixture until smooth. (Mixture will be thick.)

4. Stir in chocolate chips and vanilla. Add eggs; beat until smooth and well blended. Pour into prepared pan.

5. Bake 25 to 30 minutes or until toothpick inserted into center comes out almost clean.

Makes 9 brownies

Strawberry Shortcake

2 **pounds strawberries, sliced**

¹/₂ **cup plus 1 tablespoon sugar, divided**

1 **teaspoon ground cinnamon**

3 **cups Gluten-Free All-Purpose Flour Blend, (page 5),* plus additional for work surface**

4¹/₂ **teaspoons baking powder**

³/₄ **teaspoon salt**

³/₄ **teaspoon xanthan gum**

³/₄ **cup (1¹/₂ sticks) cold butter, cut into small pieces**

1 **to 1¹/₄ cups half-and-half**

Whipped cream

*Or use any all-purpose gluten-free flour blend that does not contain xanthan gum.

1. Preheat oven to 400°F. Grease baking sheet or line with parchment paper.

2. Combine strawberries and ¹/₄ cup sugar in medium bowl. Mash slightly to release juices; refrigerate until ready to serve. Combine 1 tablespoon sugar and cinnamon in small bowl; mix well. Set aside.

3. Combine 3 cups flour blend, remaining ¹/₄ cup sugar, baking powder, salt and xanthan gum in large bowl. Cut in butter with pastry blender or two knives until coarse crumbs form. Gradually add 1 cup half-and-half, stirring with fork until rough dough forms. Add additional half-and-half by tablespoonfuls, if necessary.

4. Turn dough out onto floured surface. Pat into ³/₄-inch-thick layer. Cut dough with 2¹/₂-inch biscuit cutter; place on prepared baking sheet. Pat remaining dough together and cut out additional biscuits. Brush tops with additional half-and-half and sprinkle with cinnamon-sugar.

5. Bake 15 to 20 minutes or until golden brown. Remove to wire rack; cool completely. Split biscuits. Layer bottom biscuits with strawberry mixture, whipped cream and biscuit tops. Serve immediately.

Makes 6 to 8 servings

Thumbprint Cookies

1 cup (2 sticks) butter, softened

$1/2$ cup packed dark brown sugar

2 egg yolks

2 teaspoons vanilla

2 cups Gluten-Free All-Purpose Flour Blend (page 5)*

$1/2$ teaspoon salt

2 egg whites, lightly beaten

$2^1/4$ cups chopped walnuts

$1/4$ cup raspberry jam

Or use any all-purpose gluten-free flour blend that does not contain xanthan gum.

1. Preheat oven to 375°F. Line cookie sheets with parchment paper.

2. Beat butter and brown sugar in large bowl with electric mixer at medium-high speed 2 minutes or until light and fluffy. Add egg yolks and vanilla; beat at low speed, scraping side of bowl occasionally. Beat in flour blend and salt just until combined.

3. Place egg whites in shallow dish. Place walnuts in separate shallow dish. Roll tablespoons of dough into balls; dip in egg whites and roll in walnuts. Place on prepared cookie sheets.

4. Using thumb or back of small spoon, make small indentation in center of each ball; fill with jam.

5. Bake 12 to 15 minutes or until golden brown and filling is set, rotating cookie sheets halfway through baking time. Cool on cookie sheets 5 minutes. Remove to wire racks; cool completely.

Makes 2 dozen cookies

Banana-Coconut Cream Pie

Crust

- 1 **cup almonds**
- 1 **tablespoon sugar**
- $1/2$ **cup flaked coconut**
- $1/4$ **cup ($1/2$ stick) butter, cut into small pieces**
- **Pinch salt**

Filling

- 2 **bananas**
- 1 **teaspoon lemon juice**
- $1/2$ **cup sugar**
- $1/4$ **cup cornstarch**
- $1/4$ **teaspoon salt**
- 3 **cups whole milk**
- 2 **egg yolks**
- 1 **teaspoon vanilla**

Topping

- 1 **banana**
- 2 **tablespoons flaked coconut, toasted***
- **Whipped cream**

To toast coconut, spread in single layer in heavy-bottomed skillet. Cook over medium heat 1 to 2 minutes, stirring frequently, until lightly browned. Remove from skillet immediately. Cool before using.

1. Preheat oven to 350°F. Grease 9-inch pie pan.

2. Place almonds and 1 tablespoon sugar in food processor; process using on/off pulses until almonds are ground. Add $1/2$ cup coconut; pulse to combine. Add butter and pinch of salt; pulse until mixture begins to stick together. Press mixture onto bottom and up side of prepared pan. Bake 10 to 12 minutes or until golden around edge. Cool completely.

3. Slice 2 bananas; sprinkle with lemon juice. Layer on bottom of prepared crust.

4. Combine $1/2$ cup sugar, cornstarch and $1/4$ teaspoon salt in medium saucepan. Whisk milk and egg yolks in medium bowl until well blended; slowly stir into sugar mixture. Cook and stir over medium heat until thickened. Bring to a boil; boil 1 minute. Remove from heat; stir in vanilla.

5. Pour mixture over bananas in crust. Cover and refrigerate at least 2 hours or until ready to serve.

6. Slice remaining banana; arrange on top of pie. Sprinkle with 2 tablespoons coconut and top with whipped cream.

Makes 8 servings

Cranberry Pear Cobbler

Filling

- 3 **pounds ripe pears (about 6 pears), peeled and sliced**
- 1$\frac{1}{2}$ **cups cranberries**
- $\frac{1}{4}$ **cup granulated sugar**
- 1 **tablespoon cornstarch**
- 1 **tablespoon grated orange peel**
- 1 **teaspoon ground cinnamon**

Topping

- 1 **package (about 15 ounces) gluten-free yellow cake mix**
- 1 **cup low-fat buttermilk**
- $\frac{1}{2}$ **cup (1 stick) butter, softened**
- 2 **teaspoons vanilla**
- 1$\frac{1}{2}$ **tablespoons packed brown sugar**
- 1$\frac{1}{2}$ **tablespoons granulated sugar**
- **Whipped cream (optional)**

1. Preheat oven to 400°F. Spray 13X9-inch baking dish with nonstick cooking spray.

2. Combine pears, cranberries, $\frac{1}{4}$ cup granulated sugar, cornstarch, orange peel and cinnamon in large bowl; toss to coat. Pour into prepared baking dish.

3. Bake 20 minutes or until bubbly.

4. Meanwhile, beat cake mix, buttermilk, butter and vanilla in large bowl with electric mixer at low speed 30 seconds or until moistened. Beat at medium speed 2 minutes.

5. Remove baking dish from oven. Pour topping evenly over filling. Sprinkle with brown sugar and 1$\frac{1}{2}$ tablespoons granulated sugar.

6. Bake 30 to 35 minutes or until topping is golden brown. Serve warm with whipped cream, if desired.

Makes 8 servings

Cherry Cheesecake Swirl Bars

Crust

1^2/$_3$ cups gluten-free
shortbread cookie crumbs

^{1}/$_2$ cup (1 stick) butter, melted

^{1}/$_4$ cup sugar

Cheesecake

2 packages (8 ounces each)
cream cheese, softened

^{1}/$_2$ cup sugar

3 eggs

^{1}/$_2$ cup sour cream

^{1}/$_2$ teaspoon almond extract

3 tablespoons strained
cherry preserves, melted

1. Preheat oven to 325°F.

2. Combine cookie crumbs, butter and ^{1}/$_4$ cup sugar in medium bowl; mix well. Press crumb mixture onto bottom of 9-inch square baking pan. Bake 10 minutes or until set but not browned. Cool completely.

3. Beat cream cheese in medium bowl with electric mixer at medium speed until fluffy. Add ^{1}/$_2$ cup sugar; beat until smooth. Add eggs, one at a time, beating well after each addition. Add sour cream and almond extract; beat until well blended. Pour evenly into prepared crust.

4. Drizzle melted preserves in zigzag pattern over cheesecake batter. Drag tip of knife through jam and batter to make swirls.

5. Place pan in 13X9-inch baking dish; add water to come halfway up sides of cheesecake.

6. Bake 45 to 50 minutes or until knife inserted 1 inch from edge comes out clean. Cool completely in pan on wire rack. Cover and refrigerate 2 hours or until ready to serve.

Makes 16 servings

Chocolate Marble & Praline Cheesecake

Crust

2 cups gluten-free shortbread cookie crumbs

$^1/_2$ cup finely chopped toasted pecans*

6 tablespoons ($^3/_4$ stick) butter, melted

$^1/_4$ cup powdered sugar

Cheesecake

3 packages (8 ounces each) cream cheese, softened

1$^1/_4$ cups packed light brown sugar

3 eggs, lightly beaten

$^1/_2$ cup sour cream

1$^1/_2$ teaspoons vanilla

1 square (1 ounce) unsweetened chocolate, melted

20 to 25 pecan halves ($^1/_2$ cup)

Gluten-free caramel ice cream topping

To toast pecans, spread in a single layer on ungreased baking sheet. Bake in preheated 350°F oven 8 to 10 minutes or until fragrant, stirring occasionally.

1. Preheat oven to 350°F.

2. Combine cookie crumbs, chopped pecans, butter and powdered sugar in food processor; pulse until combined. Press onto bottom and up side of ungreased 9-inch springform pan. Bake 10 to 15 minutes or until lightly browned. Cool completely on wire rack.

3. Beat cream cheese in large bowl with electric mixer at medium speed until fluffy. Beat in brown sugar until smooth. Add eggs, sour cream and vanilla; beat just until blended. Remove 1 cup batter to small bowl; stir in chocolate.

4. Pour plain batter into prepared crust. Drop spoonfuls of chocolate batter over plain batter. Run knife through batters to marbleize. Arrange pecan halves around edge.

5. Bake 50 minutes or until set. Cool completely in pan on wire rack. Cover and refrigerate 2 hours or until ready to serve. Drizzle with topping.

Makes 12 to 16 servings

Coconut-Lemon Layer Bars

Crust

1 **cup gluten-free shortbread cookie crumbs**

$^1/_2$ **cup (1 stick) butter, melted**

Filling

1 **package (8 ounces) cream cheese, softened**

Grated peel and juice of 1 lemon

1 **egg**

2 **tablespoons sugar**

1 **cup (6 ounces) white chocolate chips**

1 **cup sweetened flaked coconut**

$^1/_2$ **cup chopped macadamia nuts**

1. Preheat oven to 350°F. Spray 13X9-inch baking pan with nonstick cooking spray.

2. Combine cookie crumbs and butter in medium bowl; stir until well combined. Press crumb mixture onto bottom of prepared pan.

3. Beat cream cheese, lemon peel, lemon juice, egg and sugar in medium bowl with electric mixer at low speed until smooth. Spread evenly over crumb mixture.

4. Layer evenly with white chocolate chips, coconut and macadamia nuts, pressing down each layer firmly with fork.

5. Bake 25 to 30 minutes or until lightly browned. Cool completely. Cover and refrigerate until ready to serve.

Makes about 32 bars

Best Ever Apple Crisp

8 cups thinly sliced peeled tart apples

1 cup packed brown sugar, divided

1 tablespoon cornstarch

1$^{1}/_{2}$ teaspoons ground cinnamon, divided

$^{1}/_{4}$ cup Gluten-Free All-Purpose Flour Blend (page 5)*

$^{1}/_{4}$ cup cold unsalted butter, cut into small pieces

$^{3}/_{4}$ cup gluten-free old-fashioned oats

$^{1}/_{2}$ cup coarsely chopped pecans

Vanilla ice cream (optional)

*Or use any all-purpose gluten-free flour blend that does not contain xanthan gum.

1. Preheat oven to 350°F.

2. Combine apples, $^{1}/_{2}$ cup brown sugar, cornstarch and 1 teaspoon cinnamon in large bowl; toss to coat evenly. Spoon into 2-quart casserole.

3. Combine remaining $^{1}/_{2}$ cup brown sugar, flour blend and remaining $^{1}/_{2}$ teaspoon cinnamon in medium bowl; mix well. Cut in butter with pastry blender or two knives until coarse crumbs form. Stir in oats and pecans. Sprinkle evenly over apples.

4. Bake 40 to 45 minutes or until apples are tender and topping is brown. Serve warm with ice cream, if desired.

Makes 8 servings

Old-Fashioned Bread Pudding

10 slices gluten-free cinnamon-raisin bread, cut into $1/2$-inch cubes

$1/4$ cup ($1/2$ stick) butter, melted

2 cups whole milk

4 eggs

$3/4$ cup sugar

2 teaspoons ground cinnamon

1 teaspoon vanilla

$1/2$ cup raisins

$1/2$ cup chopped dried apples

1. Grease 9-inch baking dish.

2. Combine bread cubes and butter in prepared baking dish; toss to coat.

3. Whisk milk, eggs, sugar, cinnamon and vanilla in medium bowl. Stir in raisins and dried apples. Pour over bread cubes. Cover and refrigerate at least 2 hours.

4. Preheat oven to 350°F. Bake 50 to 55 minutes or until golden brown and center is set. Let stand 10 minutes before serving.

Makes 6 to 8 servings

Butterscotch Toffee Gingersnap Squares

40 **gluten-free gingersnap cookies**

6 **tablespoons (³/₄ stick) butter, melted**

1 **cup butterscotch chips***

¹/₂ **cup pecan pieces**

¹/₂ **cup chopped peanuts**

¹/₂ **cup milk chocolate toffee bits**

¹/₂ **cup mini semisweet chocolate chips**

1 **can (14 ounces) sweetened condensed milk**

1¹/₂ **teaspoons vanilla**

Read labels carefully as not all butterscotch chips are gluten-free.

1. Preheat oven to 350°F. Line 13X9-inch baking pan with foil, leaving 1-inch overhang. Spray with nonstick cooking spray.

2. Place cookies in food processor; process until crumbs form. Measure 2 cups.

3. Combine 2 cups crumbs and butter in medium bowl; mix well. Press crumb mixture evenly onto bottom of prepared pan. Bake 4 to 5 minutes or until light brown around edges.

4. Meanwhile, combine butterscotch chips, pecans, peanuts, toffee bits and chocolate chips in medium bowl. Whisk condensed milk and vanilla in small bowl; pour over warm crust. Sprinkle with butterscotch mixture, pressing down gently.

5. Bake 15 to 18 minutes or until golden and bubbly. Cool completely in pan on wire rack. Remove foil; cut into bars.

Makes 3 dozen bars

White Chocolate Pudding with Crunchy Toffee Topping

¹/₄ **cup sugar**

¹/₄ **cup cornstarch**

¹/₄ **teaspoon salt**

2 **cups reduced-fat (2%) milk**

³/₄ **cup whipping cream**

7 **squares (1 ounce each)**
   white chocolate, chopped

2 **teaspoons vanilla**

Crunchy Toffee Topping
(recipe follows)

1. Combine sugar, cornstarch and salt in medium saucepan; mix well. Slowly whisk in milk and cream. Bring to a boil over medium heat, stirring constantly. Reduce heat; cook and stir 2 to 3 minutes or until mixture is thickened.

2. Remove from heat; stir in white chocolate and vanilla until white chocolate is completely melted. Spoon into six dessert dishes. Cover and refrigerate 1 hour or up to 2 days.

3. Prepare Crunchy Toffee Topping. Sprinkle over pudding just before serving.

Makes 6 servings

Crunchy Toffee Topping

¹/₂ **cup sugar**

¹/₄ **cup light corn syrup**

1 **cup sliced almonds**

2 **teaspoons butter**

¹/₂ **teaspoon baking soda**

¹/₂ **teaspoon vanilla**

1. Spray 10-inch square sheet of foil with nonstick cooking spray.

2. Whisk sugar and corn syrup in small microwavable bowl. Microwave on HIGH 4 minutes. (Mixture will be light brown in color.) Stir in almonds and butter; microwave on HIGH 2 minutes. Stir in baking soda and vanilla. (Mixture will foam.)

3. Spread mixture in thin layer on prepared foil; cool completely. Break into pieces.

Dark Chocolate Raspberry Bread Pudding

8 slices gluten-free bread, cut into $\frac{1}{2}$-inch cubes

$\frac{1}{4}$ cup ($\frac{1}{2}$ stick) butter, melted

2 cups whole milk

4 eggs

$\frac{3}{4}$ cup sugar

1 teaspoon vanilla

$\frac{1}{2}$ cup raspberries

$\frac{1}{2}$ cup bittersweet or semisweet chocolate chips

1. Grease 9-inch baking dish.

2. Combine bread cubes and butter in prepared dish; toss to coat.

3. Whisk milk, eggs, sugar and vanilla in medium bowl. Pour over bread cubes. Cover and refrigerate 2 hours.

4. Preheat oven to 350°F. Sprinkle raspberries and chocolate chips evenly over bread mixture.

5. Bake 40 to 50 minutes or until golden brown and center is set. Let stand 10 minutes before serving.

Makes 6 to 8 servings

30